the best of james taylor

Alfred Music
P.O. Box 10003
Van Nuys, CA 91410-0003
alfred.com

ISBN-10: 0-7579-1467-5
ISBN-13: 978-0-7579-1467-6

Album Art: © 2003 Warner Bros. Records Inc.

Contents

bittersweet 3

carolina in my mind 8

country road 16

don't let me be lonely tonight 20

fire and rain 24

golden moments 29

handy man 32

how sweet it is (to be loved by you) 36

long ago and far away 39

mexico 44

only a dream in rio 48

shower the people 62

something in the way she moves 57

steamroller (a.k.a steamroller blues) 66

sweet baby james 68

up on the roof 72

walking man 76

you can close your eyes 81

you've got a friend 84

your smiling face 90

BITTERSWEET

Words and Music by
JOHN I. SHELDON

6

Coda

We got a... We got a love that's bit - ter - sweet.__

Repeat ad lib. and fade

Verse 2:
Sometimes when I'm with you
It like you're just not there
When I look into your eyes
I see that thousand-yard stare.
Then you're back in love with me,
And you can't get enough.
It's rough into smooth
And smooth back into rough.
(To Chorus:)

Verse 3:
I wish that I could love you
The way you want me to.
But I'm so scared you'll pull
Out the rug, darlin', if I do.
It's cold, it's cold.
And now there's too much heat.
One minute I'm up in heaven
And the next, I'm walkin' the street.
(To Chorus:)

CAROLINA IN MY MIND

Words and Music by
JAMES TAYLOR

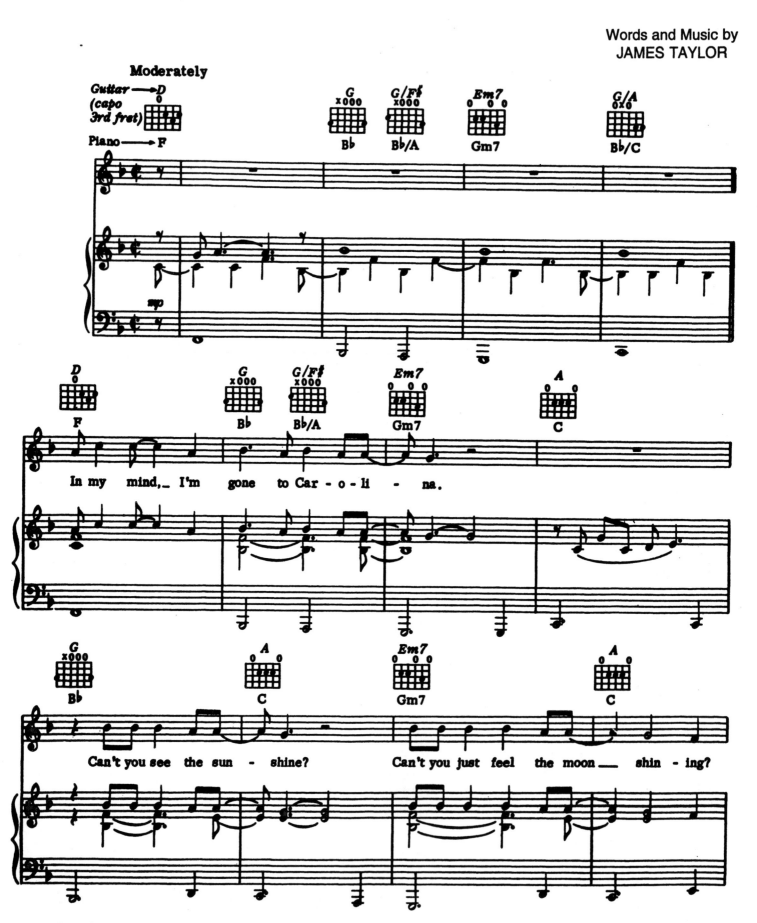

Ain't it just like — a friend — of mine — to hit me from — be - hind. —

— Yes, I'm gone to Car - o -li - na in — my mind. —

Kar-en, she's — a sil - ver sun. You'd best walk her a-way and watch — it shin - ing.

Watch her watch the morn - ing come.

COUNTRY ROAD

Words and Music by
JAMES TAYLOR

*Guitarists: Tune sixth string down to D.

Country Road - 4 - 1

DON'T LET ME BE LONELY TONIGHT

Words and Music by
JAMES TAYLOR

Don't Let Me Be Lonely Tonight - 4 - 1

FIRE AND RAIN

Words and Music by
JAMES TAYLOR

Fire and Rain - 5 - 1

Fire and Rain - 5 - 2

28

GOLDEN MOMENTS

Words and Music by
JAMES TAYLOR

Golden Moments - 3 - 1

HANDY MAN

Words and Music by
OTIS BLACKWELL
and JIMMY JONES

Hey, girls, gath-er 'round.__ Lis-ten to what I'm put-tin' down.__

Hey, ba-by, I'm your hand - y man._____

Handy Man - 4 - 1

HOW SWEET IT IS
(To Be Loved By You)

Words and Music by
EDWARD HOLLAND, LAMONT DOZIER
and BRIAN HOLLAND

LONG AGO AND FAR AWAY

Words and Music by
JAMES TAYLOR

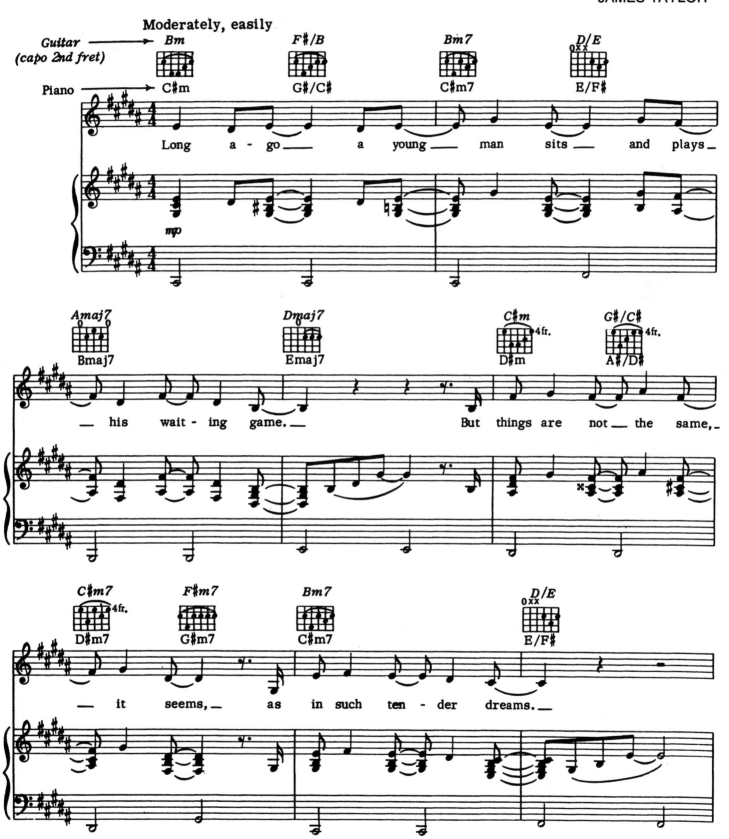

Long Ago and Far Away - 5 - 1

MEXICO

Words and Music by
JAMES TAYLOR

Way down here_

— Am - er - i - ca - no got the sleep - y eye,_ but his bod_
Ba - by's hun - gry and the mon - ey's all gone._ The folks_

you need a rea - son to move._ Feel a fool_

Mexico - 4 - 1

Mexico - 4 - 3

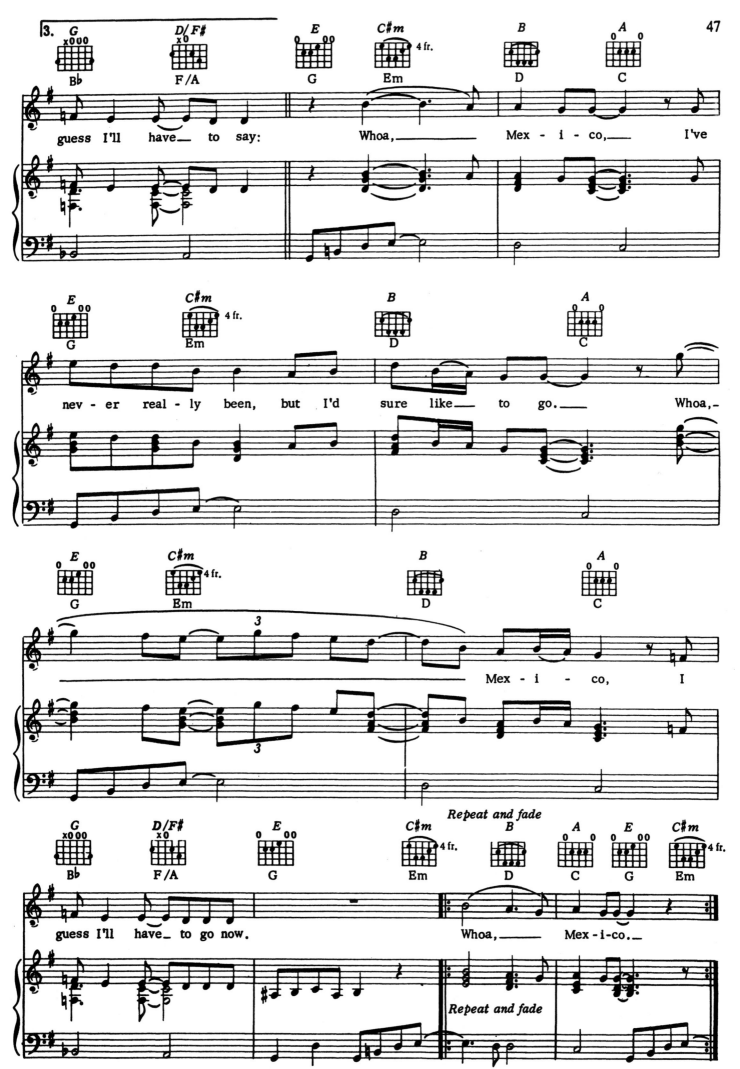

guess I'll have to say: Whoa,_____ Mex - i - co,_____ I've

nev - er real - ly been, but I'd sure like_ to go._____ Whoa,-

Mex - i - co, I

guess I'll have_ to go now. Whoa,_____ Mex-i-co._

Repeat and fade

ONLY A DREAM IN RIO

Words and Music by
JAMES TAYLOR

More than the steam - ing breeze.___
More than the con - crete Christ.___
o - ver a shin - ing sea.___
More like an - oth - er time.___

More than the hid - den hills.___
More than a dis - tant land___
More than a hun - gry child.___
More than a mil - lion years.___

1.2.3.   4.

More than a mil - lion years.___

Repeat and fade

SOMETHING IN THE WAY SHE MOVES

Words and Music by
JAMES TAYLOR

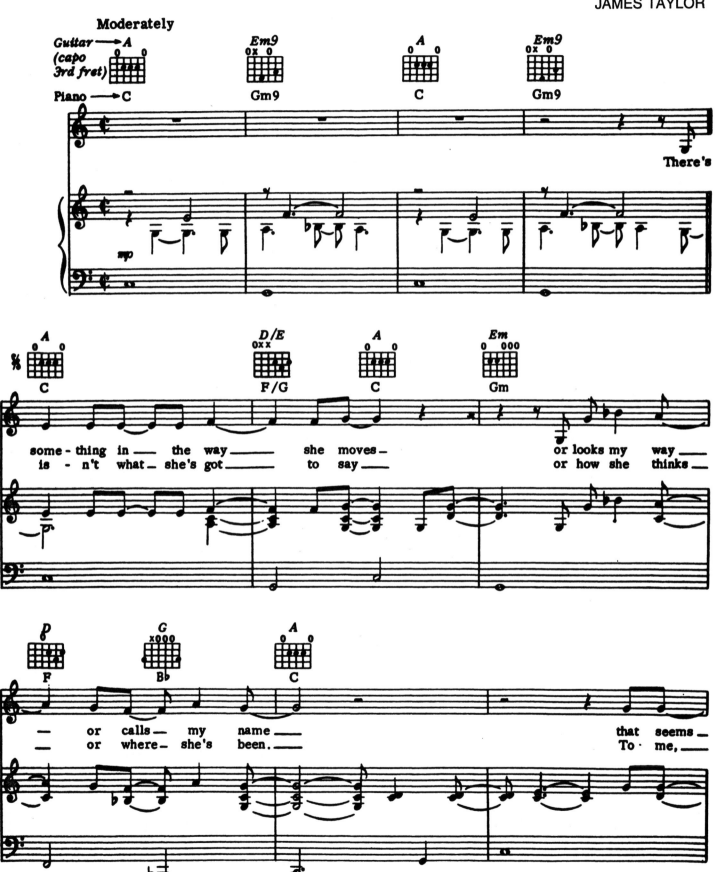

Something in the Way She Moves - 5 - 1

SHOWER THE PEOPLE

Words and Music by
JAMES TAYLOR

Shower the People - 4 - 1

Vocal Ad Lib

They say in every life,
They say the rain must fall.
Just like a pouring rain,
Make it rain.
Love is sunshine.

STEAMROLLER
(a/k/a Steamroller Blues)

Words and Music by
JAMES TAYLOR

2. Well, I'm a cement mixer; a churning urn of burning funk.
   Yes, I'm a cement mixer for you, babe; a churning urn of burning funk.
   Well, I'm a demolition derby, yeah; a hefty hunk of steaming junk.

3. Now, I'm a napalm bomb, babe, just guaranteed to blow your mind.
   Yeah, I'm a napalm bomb for you, baby, just guaranteed to blow your mind.
   And if I can't have your love for my own, now, sweet child, won't be nothing left behind.
   It seems how lately, babe, got a bad case of steamroller blues.

SWEET BABY JAMES

Words and Music by
JAMES TAYLOR

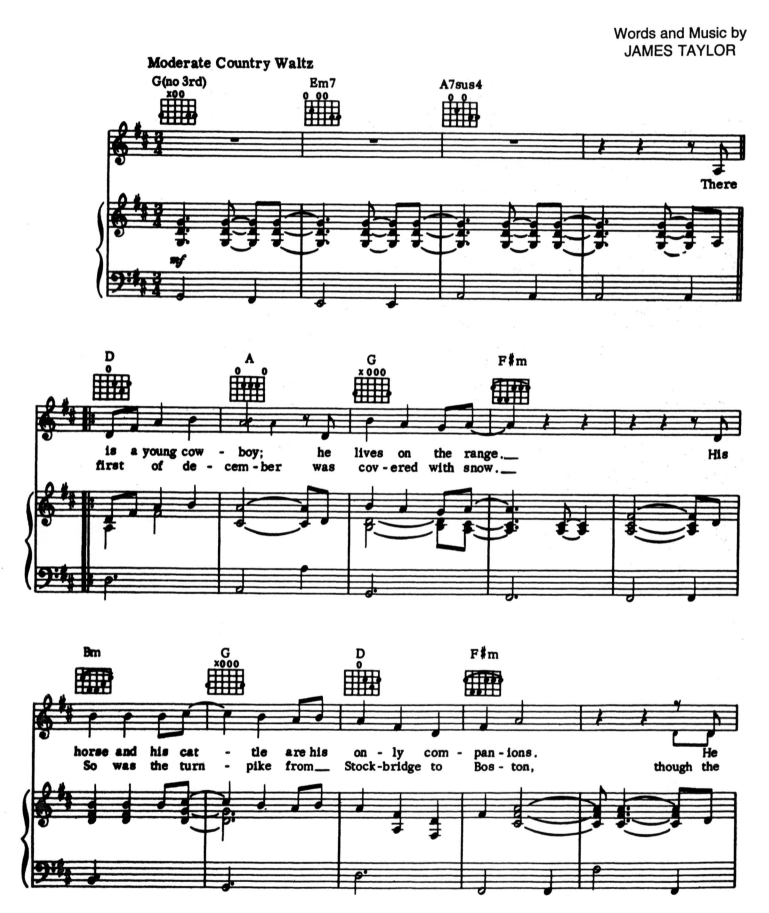

Sweet Baby James - 4 - 1

UP ON THE ROOF

Words and Music by
GERRY GOFFIN and CAROLE KING

Up on the Roof - 4 - 1

WALKING MAN

Words and Music by
JAMES TAYLOR

Moving in silent desperation,___

keeping an eye___ on the Holy Land.___

Walking Man - 5 - 1

Vocal Ad Lib

He's the walking man, born to walk,
Walk on, walking man.
Well now, would he have wings to fly,
Would he be free?
Golden wings against the sky.
Walking man, walk on by,
So long, walking man, so long.

YOU CAN CLOSE YOUR EYES

Words and Music by
JAMES TAYLOR

You Can Close Your Eyes - 3 - 1

82

YOU'VE GOT A FRIEND

Words and Music by
CAROLE KING

You've Got a Friend - 6 - 1

YOUR SMILING FACE

Moderately, with a beat

Words and Music by
JAMES TAYLOR

Tell me how much long - er; it will grow strong-er ev - 'ry day.

Oh, how much long - er? I

thought I was in love a cou-ple of times be-fore with the girl next door.

But that was long be-fore I met you. Now, I'm sure that I won't for-get

* Move capo to 4th fret.

* Move capo to 6th fret.